Entrepreneurship Ain't for Punks

Unapologetic Truths
That Spell Success
Part 1

Shar'ron Mason, MA, LMFT

Entrepreneurship Ain't for Punks
Copyright © 2021 by Shar'ron Mason

All rights reserved. No part of this book may be reproduced or transmitted in any form or by any means without written permission from the author.

ISBN (9798707175602)

Publishing: Shar'ron Mason
Cover Image: Shar'ron Mason

Dedication

Father God, You did it again. Thank You for your continued favor and provision. Thank You for entrusting me with riches for the masses. May this work be pleasing to You first and foremost.

I want to extend a sincere 'Thank you' to each and every family member and friend who has lifted prayers, spoken words of encouragement and supported me through this journey. Your love and belief in me as I fulfill my purpose means more to me than you'll ever know.

This book is dedicated to all those who are striving to build empires, brick by brick. May *Entrepreneurship Ain't for Punks* support you in aligning your thinking and habits with the greatness you're seeking.

Preface

Entrepreneurship Ain't for Punks was birthed out of a desire to support entrepreneurs, such as myself, who desire to build empires, leave legacies for the generations to come. Let's face it; it's not good enough to just have an amazing product or awesome service. It takes the right habits and mindset to be successful as an entrepreneur. It's the difference between thriving and merely surviving, throwing a celebration for your accomplishments and throwing in the towel.

In identifying the entrepreneurship-repellent attitudes, behaviors and characteristics that sabotage businesses that could be amazing, that could answer many prayers, you will be fortifying your fortress and ultimately building that legacy, that empire. Yep! I think BIG BIG!

I believe in prayer and I also believe that we are called to be the answer to someone's prayers. Some of the simplest prayers can be answered by having the financial means to meet basic and not so basic needs. I desire to do that and more. I know that I'm not the only one of this mindset.

Let's change the trajectory of your life. Let's tackle this business life together. No fluff here. Jump in. Take your inventory. Learn. Grow. Build that empire!

Introduction

Punk: a person who refuses to address the attitudes, behaviors and characteristics that make it difficult to impossible to be successful as an entrepreneur.

I'm sure you can name someone who fits my description of a punk. Guess what? *You* may be that person who comes to mind when others think of a punk with entrepreneurship-repellent tendencies. I pray that this book will help you to see yourself more clearly and I encourage you to honestly evaluate yourself as you move through these pages.

So, here's the deal, if you are able to identify and address the 15 truths presented in *Entrepreneurship Ain't for Punks*, you will be one step closer to achieving the success that you desire, that you will make the money, that you will have the impact that you desire. Ask yourself, "Do I fit the bill of the punk being described?" Brace yourself for the truth and more importantly prepare for what is to come. God can and will transform you, if you give Him room to move and come along as a partner on your journey.

Don't over think this process. If you get stuck reach out for help to address areas in which you are having difficulty grasping. As a Business Coach, I will gladly take you on as a coaching client or refer you to someone who can help you get from point A to point B. Embrace the journey. Are you ready? Let's go!

Table of Contents

Dedication	iii
Preface	v
Introduction	vii
Who is This Book For?	1
How Can You Use This Book?	3

Punks…

Have No Clear 'Why'	5
Allow Limiting Beliefs to Run Rampant	9
Operate Their Business as a Hobby	11
Lack Consistency	14
Focus on What They *Don't* Have	17
Refuse to Invest in Self	20
Lack Execution	23
Are Full of Excuses	26
Have an Unhealthy Relationship with $	29
Don't Use Networking to Their Advantage	32

Are Not In Tune with Self............... 35
Don't Level Up........................ 38
Are Ungrateful........................ 41
Get Caught Up in the Competition...... 44
Quit When the Going Gets Tough...... 47

You are Undeniably a Punk. Now What?
.... 50

Who is This Book For?

Are you just starting out on this entrepreneurial journey and wanting to be proactive in addressing any entrepreneurship-repellent attitudes, behaviors and characteristics that you possess before they cost you a lot of time and money? This book is absolutely for you.

Do you continue to find yourself stumped in your business and the reasons of 'stumpedness' continue to point to YOU, YOU, YOU? This book is for YOU.

Are you looking to go to the next level and wanting to take a look at areas that you can tweak in order to move to the next level. Yep! This books for you too!

Do you desire a Business Coach, but don't desire the financial or time commitment of that relationship? This book is for you. (I'll also be discussing the importance of the willingness to invest in yourself, so you're not totally off the hook by buying this book)

How Can You Use This Book?

There are many ways that you can use this book. You can go solo and read this book by yourself. You can read this book with others who know you well. Or you can read this book in a discussion group format.

You can read it by yourself and take note of the times that you see yourself in what you're reading. If you're self-aware or pretty insightful, this may work very well.

This book can also be read with others who know you well, such as your spouse/significant other, good friend, or accountability partner. This gives you the benefit of receiving feedback on the entrepreneurship-repellent attitudes, behaviors and characteristics that may be blind spots.

One more way that *Entrepreneurship Ain't for Punks* can be read is in a group of sorts. This could be a small cell group or book club. This will allow you to discuss the aspects of being a punk in more detail with others who also desire to nip 'punkship' in the bud, in hopes of an amazing thriving business now or in the future.

I'm sure there are other ways that this book can be used also and hey, you bought it, so feel free to use it however it'll best meet your needs. Feel free to drop me a line at lovethatrelationship@gmail.com to tell me about the ways that you've used *Entrepreneurship Ain't for Punks* for your benefit.

Punks:

Have No Clear 'Why'

Now, ain't that the truth!

Are you the Punk who has no clear 'Why'? The road to a successful business is paved with many stones of adversity and pebbles of doubt, fear, and uncertainty. Things don't always go as planned and from time to time what once felt like a well planned out strategy has to be adjusted or even scrapped. Punks don't have a clear 'Why', so they are quickly derailed and floored when these things take place.

Do you want to make a lot of money to break the legacy of poverty? Ok. Do you want to help others to feel better in a particular area of their lives? Ok. Do you want to solve a problem that people encounter simply because they're human? Ok. Embrace your 'Why' and protect it. Know it. Own it. Stand on it at all times. Because at times it will be the only thing still standing. Don't allow any and everyone else to determine YOUR 'Why'. A shaky foundation is what you'll have and we know that that won't stand.

Each of my businesses have their own specific 'Why'; however, at the beginning and end of the day it comes down to helping people to create the life that they want: with

self, with God and with others. I can live with that. I can stand on that.
Check yourself: What's your 'Why'? Is it truly your 'Why', or is it a 'Why' someone else chose for you? Can you clearly articulate it? Is it written down for you to look at from time to time? How often do remind yourself of your 'Why'?

My 'Why' keeps my flame lit and ignites others to say, YES!

Punks:

Allow Limiting Beliefs to Run Rampant

Now, ain't that the truth!

Are you the Punk that allows your limiting beliefs to run rampant? Many people can name their weaknesses far easier than they can name their strengths. This is unfortunate because we all have so much that God has endowed us with. Limiting beliefs are growth stunters and serve to diminish your self-worth and potential. Limiting beliefs plant seeds that sprout a harvest of doubt that can erect massive barriers.

When my limiting beliefs and negative self talk comes face to face with the Word of God, they are put in their place. They are annihilated. Period! "I can do all things through Christ who strengthens me." (Phil. 4:13, NKJV). My faith crushes my limiting beliefs. This may or not be the case for you. If it's not, find something that does. The one thing about limiting beliefs is that they can be so personal. They may have an ounce of truth in them or they may pull out your greatest weakness. Whatever the degree, limiting beliefs will magnify your weaknesses and attempt to destroy you internally.

Limiting beliefs can be identified by looking at your 'can'ts' then asking yourself what limiting beliefs feed your can't.

Eliminate one limiting belief at a time; whether it came from the limitations of those around you or they were placed on you by society. Naw! Give them back to whoever gave them to you and focus on the unlimited possibilities that lie within you. You've got this!

Check yourself: What are the 'can'ts' in your life that are standing in your way? Where did they come from? What does God's word say about those 'can'ts'? Is there anything that makes it difficult for you to accept God's truth?

The possibilities for my life are limitless!

Punks:

Operate Their Business as a Hobby

Now, ain't that the truth!

Are you the Punk who operates your business as a hobby? I've heard and learned that if you operate your business as a hobby, it'll pay you as a hobby. And if you operate your business as a business, it'll pay you as a business. I kid you not; I don't need another expensive hobby. What about you? If you've been slacking, make the shift to operating your business as a business, immediately.

I have had to check myself on this one (oh, and yes, my hubby has too). He asked to see my records for my newest endeavor. He ascertained that I wasn't as serious about it as my therapy work due to my lackluster way of keeping things in order. He got me all the way together when he said that somebody was going to come along wanting to invest a lot of money in me and I would lose out on that opportunity if I didn't have my stuff in order. Ouch! I'm all about opportunities so I went to work to get it together. So bring them big bucks Babee! I'm ready for you.

Check yourself: What are 2 things that you need to focus on to operate your business more like a business and less like a hobby?

What is standing in the way of you making these changes? Are you properly keeping track of inventory, cash flow, tracking trends, following up, making calls…doing the business stuff? (Get help if any of the "business stuff" is not in your wheelhouse).

I operate my business as a business and it pays me as a business!

Punks:

Lack
Consistency

Now, ain't that the truth!

Are you the Punk who lacks consistency? Lack of consistency is the downfall to many a business. I hear it all too often and shake my head because as a consumer I've definitely experienced it. Imagine going to get a meal and having the best experience ever. The food is bomb, service is on point; price is right; atmosphere is copacetic. AMAZING! The next time you go is ok. You think, well, maybe it's an off day. You go back. This time it's trash. You're like, REALLY! Some wouldn't return after that first disappointment. You might not like the sound of that, but guess what? No one has to give you another chance to earn their business. They just don't. Now, it may be a nice gesture if they do, but they owe you nothing other than compensation for the product or service received. LOYALTY? They don't owe you that. You owe them a consistently good product/service/experience. PERIOD! If lack of consistency is that one thing standing between your pretty good and your amazing, get it together, Punk!

Check yourself: How is your consistency? What are your consistency strengths and weaknesses? What do you need to do in order to consistently deliver?

I deliver consistently!

Punks:

Focus on What They *Don't* Have

Now, ain't that the truth!

Are you the Punk who focuses on what you don't have? I can't think of a time when I've wanted to do something big and had everything for the entire undertaking right there. NEVER! A prime example was when I wanted to get my Master's Degree to become a therapist. I was initially denied admission to the program, so the most basic thing that I needed wasn't even in my grasp. BUT, I had a voice to advocate for myself and guess what? The denial turned into a "well come in for an interview," which turned into a provisional admission, which turned into graduating with honors and *early* to boot (not to toot my own horn, but *Toot Toot*).

Focus on what's needed in the moment rather than what's needed to get you 10 steps ahead. It makes me think about the manna that God provided in the desert for the children of Israel. It was just what they needed for that day. The next day He provided what was needed for that day. It takes true faith to operate in this way; however, it works when we focus on what we have rather than what we don't have and focus on what's needed for the task at hand.

Some are shocked when things work out for them. I'm shocked when they don't. Ask yourself what you have in that moment and use it.

Check yourself: Do you find yourself focusing more on what you DON'T have or on what you DO have? How often do you inventory your resources, tools and connections? Do you have the Holy Spirit residing in you? If so, are you aware that He is able to teach you all things and reveal resources that you never even knew existed? (Now, tell me about what you DON'T have!)

I have all that I need to move forward in this moment!

Punks:

Refuse to Invest in Self

Now, ain't that the truth!

Are you the Punk who refuses to invest in self? Who doesn't want others to invest in them? Most people do, but when it comes time to invest into self they get really tight with their cash. Why should someone invest in you if you're not willing to invest into yourself? If you don't think you're worth the investment, why should someone else?

Investment isn't just money, but also time and other resources. Show me what you've invested in and I'll tell you what you have faith in, what you value. Look around at the folks who are truly successful in their field. I guarantee you that they've invested in themselves in numerous ways.

When you attempt to hold on to the little you have oh so tightly, somehow a hole develops in your pocket and that little begins to vanish. But, it's a different story when you're willing to invest in what's important; YOU and that thing that you want to grow; YOUR BUSINESS. Never be afraid or too cheap to invest in yourself. The returns are exponential.

Check yourself: What have you invested into your business, your growth over the past 6 months? How much have you studied? Whose expertise have you sought (and paid for) in terms of mentorship, specialized training…?

I invest in ME because I believe in ME!

Punks:

Lack
Execution

Now, ain't that the truth!

Are you the Punk who lacks execution? We've all seen folks who talk a good game. They have a ton of ideas, but never seem to get them off the ground. They may make others seem small with all these ideas, but truth be told that shouldn't be the case.

Ideas naturally flow for some; however, ideas without execution are just…ideas. Some believe that they must be the one to implement their ideas. That's small thinking. An idea person may just need to connect with an implementer and VOILA, a viable business is birthed. I have notebooks of ideas. That's how my brain operates. I also have a resume of great launches, viable thriving businesses. This only means that I'm an idea person and an implementer.

We all have our strengths and business flows best when we operate in our strengths. It doesn't make me better than or worse than the person who is the idea person or the person who is the implementer. If you're willing to make adjustments in order to set yourself up for success, you're 10 steps ahead of the Punk who's stuck on doing it the way that they see it played out in their head. Don't be that Punk. Do something different if you want to see something different.

Check yourself: Are you an idea person, implementer or both? What evidence do you have that speaks to this? Who are the implementers in your circle? Who are the idea people? Who are both? Do you need to make some connections to implement your ideas? If so, with whom?

I execute my ideas through various means!

Punks:

Are Full of Excuses

Now, ain't that the truth!

Are you the Punk who is full of excuses? Your barriers may be real. They may seem insurmountable. They may be overwhelming. They are also binding and confining. Roadblocks and obstacles only unveil opportunities for creativity and ingenuity. If you get caught up in them, the 'woe is me's' will set in. Not sexy at all. I'm just saying. When you lose the excuses, limitless possibilities somehow appear. Turn those excuses on their heads and find the opportunities in them. There is an opportunity to learn, to grow, to increase your capacity, to expand your network, to stretch your imagination and tap into your creativity, to find all the reasons why you can.

Obstacles only create excuses for the visionless. Read that again. Obstacles only create excuses for the visionless. If that's you, I'm going to encourage you to lose heart. Losing heart isn't always a bad thing. If that heart is cowardice, excuse filled, negative, visionless... LOSE IT!

Check yourself: What are the excuses that are keeping you from moving forward, not doing what needs to be done in this season?

What opportunity are they revealing? What do you need to tap into in order to turn those excuses on their heads?

My vision doesn't allow me to get caught up in excuses!

Punks:

Have an Unhealthy Relationship with $

Now, ain't that the truth!

Are you the Punk who has an unhealthy relationship with money? If you don't have a healthy relationship with money it will show. Life is all about relationships. In fact, your relationship with money guides how you operate in many other relationships in your life. You will despise money while longing for it. You will sabotage your efforts to obtain money while simultaneously striving to grow your wealth.

If you're afraid of money, resentful towards it, intimidated by it or even believe that you and money will never be a part of one another's lives, you will never have the money that you could have if you related to money in a healthy way. Getting to the root of unhealthy thoughts and beliefs about money is important, but adopting a healthier mindset is even more important (we may not always know what the root is). Empowering money mantras can help you to make the shift that's needed to make money desire to be a part of your life, to make you attractive to money.

Do you see money as being fleeting, lacking, controlling, hard to hold on to, difficult to understand…? Change your view of money and make yourself a magnet for it. Attract it. Don't repel it.

Check yourself: What's your relationship with money? How do you feel about it? How do you treat it? What do you think about it? What were you told about money when you were growing up? How do you view people who have substantial amounts of money? How do you view those with very little money? Would you want to be in your possession if you were money?

Money flows to me effortlessly!

Punks:

Don't Use Networking to Their Advantage

Now, ain't that the truth!

Are you the Punk who doesn't use networking to your advantage? Networking allows you to receive the benefit of others' strengths/giftings while operating in your own strengths/giftings. When you attempt to do it all yourself you are left with your own weaknesses unnecessarily intertwined all throughout your business. Did you catch that? Unnecessarily!

Make networking as effortless as breathing, meaning go through life with the constant lens of what do you have that I need, and what do I have that you need. Sometimes it's as simple as an introduction to someone who I can benefit and/or who can benefit me. In other words, networking with you can bridge the gap between me and someone that you know that I need to know and who needs to know me.

When we recognize that we all have strengths and weaknesses it's much easier to have a networking mindset. Get your 15 sec/30 sec intro down or as some call it, your elevator speech. Take advantage of every opportunity to use it because networking will only benefit you if you use it to your advantage.

Check yourself: Are you a Networking Boss or an undercover wallflower? Do you see the value in networking? Are you aware of your strengths and your weaknesses?
Do you have a 15-30 second 'elevator' speech ready at all times? Do you need to address any fears, insecurities or pride that makes it difficult for you to connect with others?

I network as effortlessly as I breathe!

Punks:

Are Not In Tune with Self

Now, ain't that the truth!

Are you the Punk who is not in tune with self? It is easier to maintain than it is to repair. That applies to all areas of life. From our health to our cars, regular maintenance sets us up for tune ups from time to time rather than major overhauls. I see it in the therapy room far too often where self and relationships with others are neglected and then help is sought to make that thing right.

Being proactive rather than reactive is the name of the game and unfortunately many have operated in survival mode for so long that being proactive seems like a fantasy, something only possible for those privileged to operate in that way.

Checking in with yourself may be a new concept. It may seem strange and unnecessary just as getting those check-ups may seem unnecessary when you're not noticeably having any aches or pains. A check in is simply taking a minute to slow down and ask yourself how you are doing, not 'surfacy' stuff, but how you are really doing. Are you excited, anxious, sad, frustrated, happy, discouraged…? Take notice of what you are experiencing and give yourself what you need even if it requires you to reach out for help processing and getting through that space. That's what we therapists are for (SHAMELESS PLUG)

Your mental/emotional state can and will make or break your business. There isn't room to wait until you have a breakdown of sorts to look into then. You're beyond maintenance at this point and some real work will be needed. Check in with yourself often. But don't stop there. Inventory your internal and external resources (my faith is one of my priceless assets). Apply love as needed.

Check yourself: How often do you check in with yourself? Do you have a toolbox of healthy self care tools to help you to cope with difficult emotional states or do you sweep difficult emotions under a rug only to trip over them later? How would you know that it was time to reach out for professional help? Do you seek wise counsel? What are your thoughts about therapy?

I check in with myself often and apply love as needed!

Punks:

Don't Level Up

Now, ain't that the truth!

Are you the Punk who refuses to Level Up? If you're top dog in all your circles, you need new circles. Surround yourself with folks who make you elevate. My Honey had to drive this point home to me. He was getting on me about being comfortable where I was and he struck a nerve (as he often does when he's telling me what I don't want to hear).

Your circle can absolutely have folks in it at your level and even below, but it should also have folks who are at the next level that you're trying to reach and beyond that. If you're comfortable, your circle probably doesn't have the right representation.

I'm getting hungrier and hungrier by the day. I'm also getting more and more uncomfortable. That's because I'm expanding my circle and exposing myself to next level stuff. There is something about having someone close enough to touch that is achieving the stuff that dreams are made of. It makes those dreams less of a dream and more of a reality. Dreams are for sleepers. Eyes wide open here!

Check yourself: Who's in your top 10? Who's in your top 5? Are they feeding your comfort or starving it? Who do you need to add to your circle? How are you going to make that happen?

My circle encourages me to elevate!

Punks:

Lack
Gratitude

Now, ain't that the truth!

Are you an ungrateful Punk? It can be easy to see what you don't have or what isn't going well. But it's important to be intentional about seeing and acknowledging your blessings, those things that are going well. I thank my Daddy daily for all that He provides. I send the praises up and He sends even more blessings down.

When we take our blessings for granted they tend to dry up. This is the case mentally, even if it's not the case naturally. It's actually a spiritual concept that manifests itself in the natural realm. See nothing good and you'll see nothing good. Blessings flow when the gratitude shows. Count your blessings daily.

If you feel that you're a self made man/woman and owe no one for anything that you have, cords of discontent and resentment are probably interwoven throughout your every step. Work through it, process, grieve it even, and move on. Take a few minutes at the end of your day to count your blessings. It may simply mean being grateful for making it through the day.

Check yourself: Do you tend to be more of a grateful person or a 'woe is me' type person? Do you keep it so *real* that you're unable to see the blessings all around you? Do you need to be more intentional about expressing your gratitude on a daily basis?

I count my blessings daily and there's plenty to count each day!

Punks:

Get Caught Up in the Competition

Now, ain't that the truth!

Are you the Punk who gets caught up in the competition? It's good business practice to be aware of your competition. It's not good business practice to be so consumed with your competition that you're not focusing on that special thing that you have to offer. It's a balancing act and the side that you find yourself on will surely impact how you do what you do. Focusing on the competition will move you away from your 'Why' and have you operating from a 'keeping up with the Joneses type of space'. Not cute!

Don't get caught in the competition. Doing your thing with excellence, will set you apart in and of itself. Some call this staying in your own lane. I believe we should all create the lane and be the example of originality and ingenuity. Our creator did not run out of good stuff when it came to you. Tap into that good stuff and unapologetically bring it forth. Find those who want what you have and convey all the goodness about that good stuff and deliver. And do it all over again. No need to over complicate it. Do YOU!

Check yourself: Are you consumed with your competition? If so, how does it inform the way that you do business? How can you have a healthy balance of doing 'YOU' and competition awareness? What do you do well? What do you do better than anyone else? What makes you unique? Why should your identified market choose you and not your competitor?

I do my thing with excellence!

Punks:

Quit When the Going Gets Tough

Now, ain't that the truth!

Are you the Punk who quits when things get tough? Do you have sticking and staying power or do you give up and throw in the towel at the first sign of trouble? If you haven't figured it out yet, let me yell it loud for the folks in the back, Entrepreneurship Ain't for Punks! Sometimes you must make adjustments; sometimes you need to stick it out. And yes, there are even times when you need to get an outside perspective to see something that isn't obvious to you. Sometimes we need to scrap a plan and rebuild, but sometimes we need to firmly plant our feet and ride out the storm. Wisdom will help you to know the difference.

I've heard it said that if it's that hard then it's not God or it's not what God wants for me. That's not biblical. That's not truth. Read that word and see all of the difficult places that God set His people in: Building Character All Day Long! Building Faith In Him All Day Long!

We need resilience in life. We need resilience in business. It's that thing that allows you to bounce back from disappointments and adverse situations.

Getting the cheese won't necessarily be easy, but it'll be worth it.

Check yourself: Are you a quitter? What difficult things have you worked through? How do you know when it's time to adjust, seek counsel, stick it out or quit? Are you resilient and able to emotionally regulate or do you find it difficult to regulate your emotions? Are you willing to seek help with emotional regulation (if that's an issue that you face)?

I've got sticking and staying power!

You are Undeniably a Punk. Now What?

Quite simply, use the tool in your hands and deal with the Punk that's standing between you and your amazing successful business…YOU!

-Go deep into the ***Check yourself*** portion and do an honest assessment of where you're at.
-Commit to transforming the ways in which you think and behave in which are contrary to what it is that you're striving for.
-Make my mantras after each section a part of your being or better yet develop and internalize your own.
-Seek professional help if needed.

This book isn't meant to pat you on your back and to tell you how wonderful you are. This book is about addressing ways of thinking and behaving that will negatively impact your business. Having these propensities isn't the problem. The issue is when you have issues and refuse to address them. That's what makes a Punk, a Punk.

It's the refusal to address the entrepreneurship-repellent attitude, behavior or characteristic that stands in the way of the great business that you could have. It's the refusal to change, to grow, to become a better you.

You want a great business, but you're a Punk. Now what? You have two choices. You can either attack your mess head on or you can ignore it at the expense of your business. Only you can make the choice to change.

Denial is your worst enemy when it comes to your mess. Your entrepreneurship-repellent attitudes, behaviors and characteristics have probably been a part of you for so long that you've grown accustomed to them or minimized their impact on your life. You may even believe that your issues will just work themselves out. Don't fool yourself. Your mess won't go away without some work on your part. The longer you wait to address it, the worse it is going to get.

Everyone has issues. Some are big and some are small. Some are life impacting and some are so miniscule that they go unnoticed. We all have mess to deal with.

That's just a part of being human, but there is also a process that we must go through to get to the other side. I call this process, Triple A: Acknowledge, Address and Accountability.

First, you need to acknowledge your issues. Be honest with yourself. What are your shortcomings? In what ways are you a punk? As you read this book, which chapters made you say, "That sounds like me?" What changes do you need to make to become a great business woman/man? This would be a great time to ask for honest input from those close to you. Ask God to show you the areas that you need to deal with. He will take your blinders off and allow you to see yourself, maybe for the first time.

Then, you must address your mess. Begin by asking God to help you to change. Don't fool yourself by thinking that you can handle it on your own. If you could make the changes on your own, wouldn't you have done so by now? God can transform you and He can also provide you with resources to address your mess. You may need to see a therapist or seek other wise counsel. You may even need to invest in Business Coaching.

This is the work phase. It won't be easy and you will probably want to give up, but don't short-change yourself. Engage in the process and watch what will unfold.

Alright, now you need to find someone who can hold you accountable. This is someone who will call you on your mess and not take your lame excuses. This person needs to be accessible and someone that you can respect. Your accountability partner will be trusted with intimate details about you so don't take this person's role lightly.

Annihilating your inner punk will change the course of your life and improve your business prospects. It will also positively impact your community. You will become the man/woman that God called you to be and the by-product will be your ability to be a great entrepreneur. Once you've put in the work, get ready to say "farewell" to the Punk and "hello" to the new Business Savvy YOU!

www.ingramcontent.com/pod-product-compliance
Lightning Source LLC
LaVergne TN
LVHW051512070426
835507LV00022B/3066